Reflections of Sisterhood

Cindy Miller-Wiley

From Friendship to Sisterhood

Contents

Sisterhood is not determined by race or color

Cindy Miler-Wiley

DEDICATION

This book is dedicated to my bestie and ride or die friend. Vickie Johnston.

I couldn't ask for a more dedicated and committed friend than her. By my side when I was diagnosed with cancer and hyperthyroidism. Possibly a deadly diagnosis, but she always encouraged me and was forever by my side.

She and her daughter packed up my house when I got sick and didn't give it a second thought to take care of everything for me. How could you not love her?

We've shared so many things over the years, and I thank God for her every day. I wondered when I met her what brought us together and it was her craziness like me. Dressing up, and singing old songs, which we do every time we talk. And we laughed a lot.

We pretend to be best friends from down south, Esmeralda and Maggie. We do a take on Church Folks and laugh for days. She is so committed to God and her church, and I love her as my sister in Christ. She takes people in to help them out and cares for the whole world. She's my FRIEND.

Love You Always

Elder (Cindy) She never calls me Cindy (smile)

SPECIAL DEDICATION

This book is also dedicated to Cynthia, who passed away (Cid) Adams) April 2022. If I could capture the Reflections of Sisterhood and The Woman Within for her, it would be her always wanting to fit in and not knowing her true value. It took years.

Many people didn't understand the desire she had to display her gifts and talents, but God knew because He gave them to her. We know how many times you were hurt by others with words and actions, but the woman within stayed silent and just cried.

Her voice was pleasing to the ears of God, and He loved to hear her sing to Him.

We knew how you loved to dress and could wear the sharpest shoes. Please forgive us for any

iv

hurt or harm we caused because we misunderstood who you were in Christ and never told you. Now that you are at rest, we pray that you are left with peace in your heart for your family and those you loved. We miss your flair.

Too often, we as women sometimes become jealous or envious of another person's gift. Of course, we won't admit it, but God has a way of letting you know your actions are not pleasing to him. Check yourself and your motives. If any of those traits dwell within you, ask God to remove them to become the person He intended you to be. It's called self-examination. As I stated before, there is only one you. Fearfully and wonderfully made. To God Be the Glory. Thanks, Cid, for the sisterhood!!

~Cindy Miller-Wiley~

Acknowledgements

For all the women who have passed through my life and have added nuggets along the way, I acknowledge you and thank you.

Special mention: Caron Drummond, Cynthia Brown, and Myia Romey.

Thanks for the Sisterhood!

About the Author

Cindy was born to the late George W. and Edith I. Miller. She is the youngest of 12 siblings, with only one sister still living.

She has been writing since she was 10 years old when she won her first school competition.

Cindy is the proud mother of one daughter, Dawn, and has three grandchildren Deija, Des'ree, and Devon. Her great-grandchildren are Nyi, Raylynn, Raelle, Reign, and Rue.

Cindy stated that she writes under the guidance of the Holy Spirit, not man. She believes that the greatest gift God has given her is the inspiration and encouragement to write for others.

She loves to travel and can't wait to go on a book tour.

Cindy considers herself blessed to be a blessing.

Cindy showcased her book, Life After the Diagnosis, last year in London, Frankfurt, Germany, and at the LA Book Festival.

Look out for her upcoming book

I REPRESENT POSSIBILITIES

Preface

I couldn't ask for a better Reflection of Sisterhood than my own. I am the youngest of 5 sisters and 4 brothers. All bring such wonderful experiences to my life.

We did such wonderful things together over the years. Baking, Cooking, Traveling, Christmas Eve parties, Thanksgiving Day dinner, and the memories go on and on.

There is always protection and even correction when necessary, but always with love. They all have their unique differences yet similarities when it comes to helping others and always being there for each other.

I cherish the stories the older sisters would tell, and we would laugh until we cried.

We played jokes on each other but knew when it was time to stop.

As each one passed away, it was difficult for me being the youngest with only one of them left, but so glad they were a part of my life and helped shape, along with my Mother's insight, a lot of who I am today.

Always thankful and grateful for my sisters,

Love you all to the moon....

Introduction

Only the Holy Spirit can reveal who the woman within really is.

So many women have graced my life (not always good), and I wanted to honor them for all that they have given me. I pray you'll find yourself in some of the snippets I've outlined.

It's okay to be down, just don't stay there. Stop saying something inside of me said to do this, that, or whatever It was, now and forever will be the Holy Spirit.

For years she has been dying inside to reveal who she really is but always afraid she would be rejected.

Did you know that the 'woman within' is the Holy Spirit? Whether you want to recognize it or not, that's who it is. The push to your destiny and your purpose, is because of the Holy Spirit. The talent and gifts you have are not because of you so don't get it twisted. It's what He has placed within you.

Did you not rise from shelters, sleeping in cars, sleeping on the street to go to audition for American Idol?

It was the Holy Spirit (The Woman Within) pushing you to who you are today. What you didn't realize was that God made you unique. Not to fit in but to stand out. There will never be another one like you. He fashioned you after His desire for your happiness, strength, and courage. He equipped you with creativity, love, and compassion for others.

Women around the world who have a story to share will one day truly step into the woman within.

I pray you enjoy the little snippets that I've captured over the years that will make you laugh and sometimes drop a tear. So many wonderful women have graced my life. Are there any in your life? Don't wait till they're gone to tell them so.+

Not every encounter was always a pleasant one as I didn't understand that the woman within was me being worked on also.

Our Pastor said to listen to their spirit as we continue to write. What great advice. I could see more spiritually than emotionally what many of these women had experienced. I pray that the snippets will be enlightening, encouraging, inspirational, and helpful on your journey.

Know this. God can do anything but fail. We are all vessels of clay and a work in progress.

These two items are ongoing till we leave this earth. Aren't you glad that He never gave up on you? Reach up and grab what He has for you. Believe and receive. Bless the name of the Lord!

Thanks for the Sisterhood!!

How great you are. Glory to the Lamb of God!! If there ever was a time to find and know the woman within, (The Holy Spirit), it's now!!

No more wasting time and waiting. It's today!

In 2020, we elected the first Black/Asian American woman to be Vice President of the United States. I sent her a tee shirt, "You're My

Sista and I've Got Your Back." She responded with a wonderful card to thank me.

History!

We had the first young black National Poet, Laurate, read at the inauguration of President Biden.

And now, there's a possibility of having the first Black/Asian American become President of the United States. Only God knows.

Thanks for the sisterhood

The Lord will be your confidence and will
keep your foot from being caught.

Proverbs 3:26

FOREWARD

I was doing some reflections on my life and my sisterhood with friend's past and present. I realized that many experiences in my life were about my insecurities and about not loving myself.

Not everyone will be honest about themselves, but my Dad used to tell us, "To Thine Own Self Be True'.

Many of us were born with both parents, sisters and brothers and a dog. I was, too, but my Mom didn't live long enough for me to get to know her. I didn't get a chance to talk with her about how differently I see things. Things I wanted to do, how I wanted and love to write. I miss that part of my life!

My sisterhood friends weren't always pleasant people to be around. Some of my friends were self-motivated, and others were downright mean.

How could I give up who I was for who they were just to fit it? It was the worst mistake I have ever made in my life.

If I could leave any one single item in this book, it would be to always, always, always love yourself and who God made you to be.

NO ONE CAN MAKE YOU FEEL INFERIOR,

UNLESS YOU LET THEM.

ELEANOR ROOSEVELT

LOVE YOURSELF

IF YOU DON'T REALLY LOVE YOURSELF

HOW DO YOU THINK OTHERS WILL

IF YOU DON'T LIKE THE WAY YOU LOOK

HOW DO YOU THINK OTHERS FEEL

WHEN YOU LOOK IN THE MIRROR

AND CAN'T SEE THE BEAUTY WITHIN

YOU CAN'T BLAME ANYONE BUT YOURSELF

YOU ARE YOUR OWN BEST FRIEND

LOVE YOURSELF NO MATTER WHAT

AND NO MATTER WHAT OTHERS SAY

THE GIFTS YOU HAVE ARE YOURS ALONE

USE THEM TO THEIR FULLEST EVERY DAY.

LOVE YOURSELF~

13

Thanks for the sisterhood!!

13

Mary

You couldn't ask for a more beautiful person than my sister-in-law. She has been there for me since I was 10 years old when I first met her. Always in my corner, always had my back, and took care of my daughter when I had to travel for my company. She wiped my tears, guided me through my disappointments, and loved me for who I was.

She and my brother were together for over 30 years. They had 5 children. One passed away several years ago, but her faith in Jehovah helped her make it through some tough times. She lost my brother, two brothers who passed away, her father, and her mother.

She was a very intricate part of my life as my brother took me with him whenever he went to see her, and I became a part of her family. What a joy. She was another older sister providing guidance and love for me. She will always be special to me for all that she's done for me and my family. She is very unique, and the reflections of sisterhood have shown over and over again in my life because of her. She is my sister-in-law.

If you have a sister-in-law as special as she is, make sure you let her know.

Love you much, Mary. Thanks for the sisterhood!!

Lani & Destiny

These two sisters have enriched my life with their commitment and dedication to the church and their faith in God.

One is presently a student in High School and an entrepreneur making her own cookies and sticky buns. They are very delicious.

The other sister is a student at Kutztown University and carries a dean's list average through all of her classes. She has begun her third year this Fall.

She is active in church activities, and works part-time, and they both love the Lord.

They both serve in the sound room at their church, and whenever you seek their help, they never tell you 'No'.

It is such a delight to see them grow in grace and continue their journey for Christ.

I'm so glad I met them and continue to see them grow in Christ.

Thank you both for the sisterhood!!

If you can't be kind with your words

Be quiet....

Anon.

Irie

Young and gifted, she has had a very difficult life at times. Past mistakes with her dad, she prefers not to call him that. Because of his abandonment and lack of interest and follow-through, she gave up on him.

That abandonment and the lack of support from other men who have passed through her life have made her bitter and resentful at times. She has, however, moved past those people and those circumstances to become the mother she is to her children. The Reflections of Sisterhood and the woman within hurts, gets disappointed, and wants to give up, but because God has purpose and destiny in her life, she has no choice but to move forward and make it.

The enemy fights her continuously and is always on her back because he has seen the greatness within her. When she steps into her purpose, she will be awesome for the cause of Christ. My prayer is that she will always know how much she is loved and cared for, not only by her mother and grandmother but by Christ alone, who cares for her deeply. I love her dearly.

GOD IS MY REFUGE AND STRENGTH, AN
EVER-PRESENT HELP IN TIMES OF
TROUBLE

PSALM 46:1

Pastor Val

I met her many years ago and she has been an encouragement and inspiration to my life. Pouring into me for years. We talk whenever God says it's time to connect and although we are in different states and at different paths in our lives, it never changes. Only gets better. God gets the glory for our connection, correction if needed, destiny, and purpose. Thank you for all you've done! TGBTG

YOU ARE FEARFULLY AND

WONDERFULLY MADE.

PSALM 139:14

There is no greater love than this, that a man would lay down his life for a friend.

Disclaimer: Some of the names have been changed to protect the innocent. Sit back and enjoy!

Dawn

This is my daughter, and I could write volumes about her. Most of all, she has blessed my life immensely. She had some struggles she had to go through, but she made it. Life has not been easy for her but she never gave up on God or herself. She may have stepped back, but she knows where her source of hope, faith, guidance, and direction lies.

She didn't want to always listen to me as her mother, and we had our ups and downs but once we got through the yukky stuff, we finally were able to be Mother and daughter.

She reminded me many times that she wanted more of my time as I was busy trying to make money so we could have a good life. I didn't realize how much it hindered her growth, especially when it came to our relationship.

I apologized for that time and we've talked many times about it. We both learned from being honest.

She has a creative spirit like me, loves helping others, loves her independence, and is an entrepreneur.

When she allows God to work in her life, she sees how successful she can be when she stays the course. I love how He continues to direct her life and her children when she allows Him in.

Never give up, and keep looking up.

There's a blessing in the pressing and stressing. Thank you for the sisterhood!!

Crystal

It will be 3 years in December since she has passed away. (December 15, 2022)

How do I describe this Woman of God? She has been such a blessing in my life and the life of many others. She was a Pastor and truly gave her all to the Lord. She came into my life at a time when I needed and wanted to see God's glory within His people. She was that person. Her persona exemplifies His grace, mercy, love, faith, and so much more.

When I had to have surgery for cancer in 2010, she and another friend of mine came to pray with me. We were praying so hard that the security guard came in to make sure everything was ok. It was, of course. But the Holy Spirit was in that place at the time, and we called on heaven for my surgery, recovery, the surgeons, and for God's hand to be on everything the next day. We were crying, shouting, and more crying as we were all so full. I felt honored that she came to pray with me, and I thank God for using her to bless my life. She was a wonderful friend who truly loved the Lord and was a wonder in the eyes of our Lord and Savior. Bless you, sis, and all that you put your hands on. Although we didn't see each other often, you were in my prayers, and He knew when we needed to connect. Love you much. Don't forget to remember those people who have touched your life. Won't He Do It. Sadly missed, but never ever forgotten. Thank you for the sisterhood!!

Beth

Some women don't like exposing their inner selves, but it is rewarding when you take a look at the mistakes, disappointments, and bad decisions and move past them.

This is Beth. She made a lot of bad decisions, picked the wrong men to get involved with because of low self-esteem, and was always settling.

She had several children, but she was a good mother. Just not good at picking the right man. She went through years of this until one day, she woke up and got herself together for herself and her children. She had been in an abusive relationship but got her head together as her children were growing up and were soon to begin their own lives. It was difficult for her, but she had a deep longing to do and be better. What was she going to do? She dug deep down within herself, had to move numerous times, continuously ran out of money for rent, prayed a lot, asked for direction and guidance, and found the woman within. Her mother is a praying mother and wants nothing but the best for her children. She didn't realize who she was in Christ. She and her mother didn't always see eye to eye as she had an addictive past. It's hard becoming who God wants you to be because the enemy is fighting you every step of the way. It was hard, but she was determined to make it. She still has milestones to overcome. But my God from Zion, once you decide to turn that thing around and start to depend on Him, things begin to happen in your life. He will pour out a blessing you won't be able to handle. You have the power to step on serpents' heads as God declared in his word. Have a want to spirit and see what happens. Just tell Satan. Not today; you are under my feet. So, girl, get to stepping!! Be blessed! Thank you for the sisterhood!!

Do the best you can until you know better.

Then, when you know better, do better.

Maya Angelou

Annie

Her name was Annie and she had fallen into hard times. She got pneumonia. She had no health insurance as she had just started a new job. She wasn't eligible for welfare, had no money, and wasn't able to pay her rent, which had gotten months behind. She didn't want to go to her family for help because she wanted to do it on her own and not hear them talk about her. You know. You've been there. And she didn't want to go to her church for help.

One day, when she came home from work, there was an eviction notice on her door stating that she needed to be at the District Justice Office on August 16, 2006. She panicked, not knowing what to do. She cried first, began to pray, and then called her BFF.

She explained everything that had happened, and they prayed together. Her BFF said she would go with her to the DJ's office and reassured her that all was in God's hands.

As the date approached, she was beside herself with anxiety as she didn't have anywhere to go, and how would she come up with $2395. She cried more but continued to keep a good smile although she was dying inside. You know, like we do.

They went to the DJ's office, where her landlord presented his case, and she had no recourse because she knew she was behind.

The DJ told her that she had 20 days to get the money together or she would be evicted. Why do we wait till the last minute to respond or to ask for help when we already know that we are behind on bills? Then we get mad when the resources that are available can't help you.

As they left the DJ's office, they both were in tears as to what Annie was going to do.

They went to church on Sunday and laid it all on the altar.

Annie went home after church, and the phone rang. It was her landlord's wife. She said, "Annie, my husband and I have been talking. We have decided to forgive the money ($2395) you owe us." Annie responded, "Oh my God." The landlord's wife said my husband has been diagnosed with cancer, and all we want you to do is pray for him and start a new beginning." Annie was so elated she didn't know what to do. She thanked her and told her she would do exactly what she instructed her to do. The Holy Spirit had touched her landlord's heart. My God!

She called her BFF, and they screamed, and praised God, and Annie gave her testimony the next time she went to church. But the response wasn't what she expected. She expected everyone to be happy for her about how God had blessed her, but that response never came. There were some who said that was great, but many others who said nothing. You can't count on others for your happiness or success.

The woman within knew there was nothing God wouldn't do for us when we needed Him to intervene on our behalf. She wanted to scream from the rafters -- is anything too hard for God? When you trust and believe, 'won't He do it'. The sisterhood between them was unbelievable. Be blessed!

No one knows all the ins and outs
No one knows all your pains and doubts
No one knows the hurt behind the grin
Only Jesus knows the woman within.

The woman outside is strong and sure
She knows what to do and when to do it
She has no doubts is assertive and sharp
But no one but Jesus knows the pain in her heart.

On her knees every night she spends time
with her God
She laughs, she cries, she moans, she fights,
she asks the Lord, please help to survive
Then the Lord comforts and strengthens the
woman inside.

You're there for a reason I've chosen this place
This temple is in ruin. The people are
disgraced
I need you to stand against evil and sin
I'm placing my power in the woman within,

So go forth my dear daughter don't get tired
or weak
I'm here when you need me my guidance to
seek
Go forth my sweet soldier, I'm there to the end
Just hold to the spirit of the woman within.

LET GO OF ENVY

SO, THE WOMAN WITHIN CAN

COME FORTH

Jadesa

Her name is Jadesa, and she has a heart of love. We met almost 20+ years ago.

We hit it off immediately as friends because we had like spirits. Be careful of the people you call your "friends" and ask the Lord, is this someone you want in your life. He'll let you know. Don't go on your emotions. They'll get you in trouble.

She will do anything she can for anyone, especially her family.

She is a good, true, honest, all-or-nothing friend.

Do you know someone that reminds you of Jadesa?

She worked hard all her life. 35 years of employment and finally retirement.

She loves her church and is very committed.

The one part of Jadesa that this little snippet wants to bring to your attention is her heart of love.

Several years ago, she had two occasions that could have taken her life, but God. She got shot, was in a car accident, and was diagnosed with cardiomyopathy. She picked herself up, dusted herself off, and went on with her life. As she would say, "I've got to be here for my kids and my grands." I've got much to do for them and the kingdom.

Life for her wasn't always easy as she grew up in a dysfunctional family, as many of us do but won't admit it. Her grandmother raised her and taught her values about life, how to treat others, and how to make it. Her grandmother had her own hair business and was very successful. But the woman within knows the truth. Every now and then, she reveals a little more of the woman within. Her bouts of disappointments, her low self-esteem, her wanting to fit in, and more importantly, her wanting to be loved. She rose above all the negatives in her life and made them all positives. When her family hurts, she hurts. Will do anything to help them and support them.

If you knew her, you would love her. She's always positive, even when the enemy is on her back. She always points you to Christ.

She masks a lot of her pain by portraying characters she might become, i.e., a clown, a downtrodden bum, a Jamaican, and so many others. She has a heart of love.

She takes in strangers who need a place to stay for a few days, weeks and, yes, sometimes months. She's always trying to find ways to help someone else on this journey. She always makes herself last. She has a heart of love.

For her, the woman within and sisterhood is dealing with the truth, digesting all the garbage, and giving it to God. Being all that God has promised her would be difficult for her at times, but it doesn't change her heart of love.

I'm so glad to have her in my life. She is my confidante, my road buddy, my character dress-up partner. She is my friend. She has a heart of love.

There are so many stories I could share about her, but if you have a Jadesa in your life, cherish her. For there's only one Jadesa, and she has a heart of love. Be blessed. Thank you for the sisterhood

Marge

She's strong in her own right, but due to many medical problems in her life, she was often misunderstood, especially by those that she loved and respected the most.

The doctor labeled her bipolar. God labeled her blessed and found her highly favored. He called her beautifully and wonderfully made by Him. She is precious in His sight.

The disability she had hovered over her life for many years. At times, she would become depressed while also caring for her grandchildren and mother. But Marge trusted and believed that God would bring her through any situation, and He did just that.

She completed beauty school and other courses. She opened her own business and then went into business with her daughter, operating a daycare center.

Many take her for granted because of her quiet nature and kindness. She is a jewel. She loves the Lord, her husband & family, and church. She's growing more and more in Christ on this journey and never forgets where God has brought her. He is her strength. How's your journey? Are you being honest with the woman within? She has overcome many obstacles in her life, but she's still moving. God is with her and her husband. Be blessed. Thank you for the sisterhood.

Jona

Jona is what her husband called her. You know, one of those sweet nicknames your spouse gives you. Now you're talkn' about somebody that could make homemade rolls. That was Jona. Those rolls would make you break out in a shout. She would call me every time she made them, +, just out of the oven. She was the oldest sister and let you know that. She didn't take no stuff off nobody. The woman within was grateful for her marriage, her children, her grandchildren, and her family. She served in her church, was always singing, and loved the Lord. She thought she was the boss of everyone. She loved family reunions and making history about her family. She could dress. Always had her hair and nails done. She said it was her gift to herself. She loved to travel and if she had to travel alone, she still went. She would take me on different outings so that I would feel a part of being around her daughter, having pictures taken and just having fun. Whenever her daughter would come in to visit, I would always make her put on pants so we could play outside. She hated it because she liked being dressed up. When she had a stroke, it was so heartbreaking for me, but she bounced back for a short period of time until she passed away. She was truly loved. Thanks, Ion. Thank you for the sisterhood!

Edie

She was wonderful. Not educated by man's standards, but a wonderful mother of 12. She was adopted and treated horribly by her family because of the color of her skin. Can you imagine back in 1905, racism was alive and well amongst our own people? She was much browner than her siblings. Her heart was kind, pure and gentle. She only knew God's love. The woman within was her greatest gift as she cared about God, family, and herself last. She loved the Lord with all of her being. She was focused on nothing except her relationship with God, her husband, and her children. She would sit and pray for hours in her rocking chair after dinner was done and the kids were taken care of. She left the discipline to her husband. Her hair was long and beautiful, and my dad loved it. They said on many occasions that they would rather she disciplined them than our dad. She loved her husband beyond the moon. He was the breadwinner, and she was his queen. She married very early in life and only knew one man, her husband. The woman within was happy and content with loving the Lord. Often, she would hand people going through our alley food if they were hungry. But that was her kind heart. Everyone loved her.

They called her Miss "I". Before she passed away at 45, she prayed and asked God to take care of her children. Especially her baby, who was 2 when she left. I thank God that He instilled her kindness towards others in all of us. We never forget about others. Sometimes, we get hurt because we care so deeply, but we know who has

all the answers. He honored her request, and I

have been blessed my entire life. We celebrate her

life. Create many memories when you have a

chance. Thanks, Mom.

Pam

She had everything. Money, her own home, a great job, and had it going on. You would never know she was blessed because she never flaunted her wealth around and treated everyone fairly. Her father was a pharmacist before he passed and made sure by purchasing stocks in companies like Motorola, UGI and Bell Telephone and blessed her and her siblings with their own stock portfolio. She was very committed to her zest for travel, her dog, and her career. She never talked about God but never told me to stop talking about Him when I did. Maybe something I said during the years I've known her touched her life. She gave me my first break at being a professional at Hershey Chocolate Company and I've never forgotten. We haven't spoken to or seen each other in over 20 years. She moved to Michigan, and I tried to locate her but didn't know if she had married and had a different name. However, my prayers are always with her. Maybe someday we'll see each other again. Thank you for believing in me. Thank you for the sisterhood.

Ruth

What a wonderful person she is. Would give you the shirt off her back, full of fun until she suffered several falls years ago and never got out of bed again. I cherish her and her life and how she's helped so many people. She is a good friend, and loves the Lord, but her best friends have passed, so now she relies on God and her family. She has some symptoms of Dementia, but at other times, she is sharp as a tack. She doesn't complain and is still very witty with a smart mouth to those who visit. She can't believe she has lived so long, but I remind her who I am and the memories we share. How sad it makes me not to see her cooking and baking and she could cook. She could make a chicken scream when she used to cook. Her sweet potato pie would make you slap your momma. She retired early after she worked 25 years at a local hospital.

If it had not been for her, I don't know what I would have done when I had gastric cancer. The woman within knew what to do as we prayed, and she sang to me each night for almost a year, which allowed me to make it through today. What a wonderful, loving sister. Life wasn't easy for her. She had to quit school to take care of the younger children in her family, and she wasn't happy about that, but that's what they did in those days. She had a dysfunctional marriage who didn't see her value, but she rose above that to go to nursing school and become a nurse for over 25 years. I love her to the moon!! Thank you for the sisterhood!

Jenny

Could skate, bake coconut cake, and just enjoy her life. She loved her children, grandchildren, and her dog, Sandy. She was very active in her church, singing in the choir and teaching Sunday school. She was loved by many who knew her. She left a legacy of always playing tricks on others and doing mischievous things to her other sisters. Especially her oldest sister. Loved to scare her. She was the jokester in the family. She was a good friend and loved the Lord. Although she had health issues, she never stopped helping when someone needed help if she could. She loved being around her sisters and brothers at holiday times and eating chicken wings like there was no tomorrow. What legacy are you leaving for your family? She was our historian. She was loved. Thanks for the sisterhood!

Kadesha

As she called 9-1-1, her face badly bruised and swollen with blood running from her nose, she said to the operator, "I would like to order a pizza, a pepperoni pizza, so the operator would know her life was in danger. She gave the address so they would dispatch the police. 9-1-1 operators had been trained when they heard those words to immediately dispatch the police. My God. She didn't recognize her value and didn't know how to get out. The woman within (the Holy Spirit) kept telling her to leave, but she wouldn't because she loved him. This went on for years until one night, after he had beaten her so badly, she decided to take her life. This wasn't a life anymore, and she had lost all of her strength to fight. If she only knew all she had to do was listen to the still quiet voice in her spirit to leave and that He would be with her. But she didn't know, and had not been taught about the Holy Spirit, so she gave up. Don't let this happen to you. God is able to do anything but fail. At your lowest, he will lift you up if you just trust and believe. Her suffering was over as her family laid her to rest, but the cost of the oil in her life was priceless. To God Be the Glory!! It's never too late to walk away. Thank you for your sisterhood!

Marie

She was a very loving mother to her children and certainly loved the Lord. She was always willing to help others as her mother raised her. She lost a son very tragically, which hurt her deeply. A mother knows her children. Do you? The woman within accomplished many things in her life until she became ill. She never gave up on Jesus and never gave up on her children. She had some difficult times in her life but always rose above those times. She was truly loved and missed by her family and friends. Thank you for the sisterhood!

When I pray
Things begin to happen
God hears my humble cry
He looks inside my heart
But already knows the reason why.
He says, daughter
Don't you trust me
What do I have to do?
To show you I'm always with you
As I've shown you many times
How much I love you.
I feel your tears of sorrow
As you cry out to me
But shouldn't you already know
To just rest and trust in me.

Reene (Pronounced Ree ne)

The cost of someone's oil is like telling their story about themselves. She was not an easy person to get to know or get along with. She seldom spoke unless it was in a condescending manner. Very seldom did you see her smile. She was in her own world about her and her family. She didn't reach out to anyone who wasn't in her circle of acquaintances. She was in a leadership role, but who would want to emulate what they saw? No one!!

Her and I butt heads all the time and barely spoke in the house of God. Ever been there? What a terrible place to be in ministry, and it saddens God's heart. I didn't realize her value or her worth until I preached a sermon one day about the alabaster box. I saw her drop to her knees in tears as I was preaching and saw the woman within come forth for the first time. In my spirit, God revealed that she was carrying much about her past, family issues, her husband who was ill, and where she was going in Christ. She had to keep up a façade so no one could see the real her, the vulnerable person. When I became ill, I really had an opportunity to see her as God saw her and forgive her. After that moment, we spoke all the time, we embraced because that's what we're supposed to do as children of the most high God. We don't know anyone's story unless they share it. Be careful how you form opinions of people without knowing the full story. Study to be silent. To God Be The Glory. Thank you for the sisterhood!!

Maylynn

I met her about 23 years ago, and she will always be special to me. She has a very quiet, loving spirit and would do anything she could to help someone out.

Although our friendship has gone its separate way, I will never forget her and wish her much love, joy, and peace. She has a heart of gold and although she had some disappointments in her life, she has risen above them all.

I love you like a sister. Much love to you and thank you for the sisterhood!

Yanya

I met her in 2011 when I was the Director of an Alzheimer's Unit. She was filled with the glory of the Lord the moment we began to talk in 2011. She was very special as she cared so much about every client we had in our unit. I call her my daughter from another mother. She's a wonderful mother, and businesswoman, filled with God-given ideas for the future of her children and herself.

She had many obstacles to overcome as she didn't like the way she looked. We talked about God being the best at helping us overcome any obstacles in our way. He did just that as He looked from the inside out and let her know that she was absolutely beautiful.

I'm so grateful that I met her, and although she has moved to another city, we still keep in touch as the woman within continues to come forth in her life. I wish her nothing but happiness, peace, and joy. Is there anything too hard for God? Love you!! Thank you for the sisterhood!!

Sunshine

What a breath of fresh air when I met her. Such a thirst for Christ like I hadn't seen in a long time. Her spirit is kind and loving as the woman within comes forth with power and might for the cause of Christ. She lends a helping hand anywhere she can and is a blessing to the ministry. She loves her family and loves the word. I see Jesus working in her life to give her her heart's desire. Sometimes, it can be hard because of life and life situations, but she always gives words of encouragement to everyone she meets. She always speaks the truth. Do you know your purpose and your destiny? Her walk-in ministry is a powerful one, and where He is taking her. To God Be the Glory. Do you know someone like that? Encourage them, support them. Thank you for the sisterhood!!

Dorothy

Where would I be without her in my life? I met her in 1999 at a church I was attending. The moment I saw her, I knew who she was. She prophesied over my life, and we've been friends ever since.

She came into my life at a very critical time. I was going through a divorce and betrayal and had nowhere to turn. But God -- I hadn't formed an intimate relationship with God at that time. She invited me to her home (Naomi's House) in Virginia, and what did I think I was doing going to someone's home that I didn't know (yet my spirit knew she was a prophet)? She ministered to me the entire weekend. I didn't even have money to get back home. But God. She gave me the bus fare to get home. My God, what a time. Ever been there? I cried and snotted all three days, and she wrapped me in a cloth from Africa to bring me peace. We went to the best place I can tell you that had the greatest cheeseburgers I've ever had. We laughed then, and we still laugh about it today. Not McDonald's. She made me breakfast that consisted of orange sherbet. My God. What a treat. At that moment in time, I met someone who truly cared about who I was and what I was going through. She shared some things I didn't necessarily want to know, but I heard what God was speaking through her.

I saw Jesus carrying the cross and praying when I was there, sleeping in her den. We talked for months, then years, and haven't been apart except by miles since. We've visited, and I so enjoy Alabama. There hasn't been a problem I'm afraid to share with her. Every disappointment and betrayal came with words of encouragement and scripture.

She's had her moments of setbacks and is now divorced, but God gave her a church where she's been Pastor for over 15+ years, and they love her. She worked in Hospice as a Bereavement Coordinator, and she loved it. However, they informed her that her job was ending and she had no time to prepare but she knows that God is able and He will take care of her. And He did with another Hospice organization. She is a grandmother, daughter, sister, and dearest friend. She's committed to the Lord and how He has worked in her life. Love you much. Thank you for caring for me and sharing "The Woman Within". Thanks for the sisterhood!!

Mom Williams

What a wonderful, loving person and mother.
She accepted me into her family when my brother
was dating her daughter, and they later married.
I was part of the family, and there was no
difference between me and her biological
children. Always made me feel special and loved.
There was none like her. Thank you, Mom.

Lynn

She was very surprised when she went to the doctor, who informed her that she had breast cancer. She took it on the chin but was devastated when she had to begin chemotherapy and radiation.

I shared with her what to expect as I had gone through the same regime along with surgery. They also told her that the cancer was in her bones. It took a toll on her as she lost weight and lost her hair. During this time, she lost her father, but she's been doing her best to hold on. She's the type of person who never wants you to see her cry because that would show weakness.

It's been a very difficult road but she's hanging in there. She attends church every Sunday and attends other functions when she can. Her mother and sister are very supportive and pray for her all the time. The woman within is a fighter and loves the Lord. She doesn't express herself with clapping or shouting but you can see the joy in her spirit when she talks about how far God has brought her. She's always cold, which comes with chemo, but she has a security blanket that keeps her warm at all times. She's a joy and I told her that when she's ready, she has a story inside of her that God will help her to write as He did me. She gives God all glory and honor as she continues her journey. She's walking better. Sometimes with a walker for stability, but she thinks she's grown and doesn't need any help but we're here to help her if she needs us. She just smiles and says thank you. Oh, I almost forgot. She makes the best pound cake you could ever eat. One day, she baked 5 cakes by herself because she felt she could. It's a journey for her, but she's on her way to healing. We give God all honor, glory, and praise. Don't forget to take care of your personal business. Thanks for the sisterhood!!

Althea

She was on fire for Christ until she got sick, and she still tried to do it for herself and her family. Depending on other people was not her style. She and her sister, who passed away many years ago, were like the Boppsie twins. Always together, never far from one another. Her sister and mother's death took a toll on her, and when she became ill herself, it really knocked her down. She loved the Lord with all her heart and her family. It was difficult to see her at times because she had become so fragile, but we kept her uplifted in prayer. Sometimes, she would get on the prayer line or even attend church service. What a joy.... She was a trooper and was not giving up. Not today, Satan. She had been through some very difficult times, but she always rose above with God's help and lots of prayer. We honor the woman within (holy spirit) and how he was continually watching, encouraging, guiding, and directing her. I thanked her and her sister when I was going through a difficult time, and they came to my rescue with no questions about my job. He is in the healing business, the balm in Gilead when you trust and believe. To God Be the Glory!! Thanks for the sisterhood!! Sadly she passed away in November, 2023.

Maggie

She's a very special person in my life. She used to be an employee when I had my card shop. I've missed our talks and seeing her as she travels between home and North Carolina. What a great friend who saw me through many difficult times as we travelled together to Disney, where I was called to showcase my business. We went there on a wing and a prayer, but my God provided the provisions we needed to stay there. 18 hours of driving down and 18 hours coming back and an air conditioner that broke down. My God. It was very hot, and every now and then, as we were driving, she would say, 'Do you need a squirt?' and she would squirt me with a spray bottle and we would laugh and keep going. We showcased my cards and cards given to me for others. We shared an intimate loss for her when she lost her finance' years ago to AIDS, but the woman within continued raising her son and moving forward. She was like my baby sister as we talked about everything from soup to nuts. No condemnation, just joy. When she was stricken with a brain tumor, I didn't know until I saw her at Walmart, and she told me. It brought tears to my eyes. We hugged, laughed, and caught up on what we had been doing and promised to keep in touch with each other. Don't wait until someone you care for is gone to thank them and to remember them. It's never too late. Thank you for the sisterhood!!

I used to tolerate a lot because I didn't want to lose people. Now, I establish boundaries because I don't want to lose myself.

Kathleen Diane

Real Life Reflections

Blue Mirror

How do I capture the essence of who she is? We met in 1969, and although we parted ways for a minute, we found each other again, and the friendship continues. We worked together and would go to the Blue Mirror for lunch where they would display Strawberry Shortcake in the window. Just imagine that picture. We got a piece each time we had lunch there. So delicious. She introduced me to Church's Chicken and Popeyes. My God. Her family became my family, and my family became hers. We travelled up and down the road to Virginia, looked at houses when I thought about moving there, went shopping, and just had a wonderful time as friends. My Dad appreciated who she was when she came to visit and warned her about my brother — to keep him at arm's length. She also had a brother, and they told me the same thing about him. We laughed at the similarities with each other but were always supportive. She is my daughter's godmother, and they have a unique relationship. My brother passed away first, and then her brother. It was a difficult time for us, but with God's help, we made it through and forgave each other.

I had great expectations, and I think it frustrated her because of how I was. Always expecting others to think like I thought. Wrong, wrong. They are to be who God made them to be. To meet His expectations and never mine. I learned that the hard way. It's been a long friendship, and when we were apart, it was like losing a part of myself. The woman within healed the wounds, and I thank God we're still friends. Whenever anything happened in our families, we tried to be there for each other. Death, sickness, marriages, birth of children. I forgot that as I was changing, and so was she. I didn't have to be right all the time. What an eye-opener. Bless the name of the Lord. Thank you for the sisterhood!!

Miss Bea

They called her 'Mother'. She and my dad were mutual friends many years after my mom passed away and her husband. She combed my hair and made sure I looked decent for school. He so much appreciated it as he had to work, and the other kids had to go to school, which they had to walk to. I appreciate her being a part of my life and helping me with my growth. She was truly loved by all who knew her.

82

Terri

Thank God for this gifted woman of God in my life. We met approximately 20+ years ago when we worked together at a nursing home at night. We began to share the bible and the prophetic anointing that was on her life. I told her I received prophetic utterances from the Lord and sometimes it scared me when it came to pass. But she encouraged me to just trust God and if He wants to increase the anointing in that area, He will. She loves the lord with all her heart and has a heart for Him. She loves her family, traveling, evangelizing, preaching, and teaching.

She especially loves her children and grandchildren. This is her time. God has chosen her for the nations', and she is on her way. To God Be the Glory. Her mother was her best friend, and she cared for her tenderly as only a nurse can do with the anointing of the Holy Spirit. Her mother passed recently, and her brother. It has been extremely hard on her. But we keep praying for her and her family as she continues her journey in Christ. There's no stopping her. She is so special to me, and I thank God that He has brought her back into my life. Keep your eyes on her as she is walking in total Victory in Christ. God is with you. Thanks for the sisterhood!!

Michaele

I would never call her that out of respect. She is Elder now Pastor, and I give her all the respect that is due her. What a gem for me when I was entering the ministry. She knows the bible front and back and then some. She loves riding motorcycles and, of course, her children and grandchildren. When we were in ministry at another church, she provided so much background information on the bible that you wanted to learn more and all that you could. She was a blessing to my life when I was in a car accident. She came to make sure I was ok at the hospital and stayed with me until I was discharged. Came to see me when I was in the ICU after cancer surgery. I don't remember a lot about the night or the day she came; I just know she was there. What a friend. She has moved to another city down south, and we touch base every now and then. I'm so glad that I met her and have learned from her. She loves the Lord and is committed to His cause for her life. Don't wait until life changes happen to keep in touch with your friends. No more excuses. Thank you, and I love you very much. Thank you for the sisterhood!!

Cheryl

How do I describe her? What a blessing in my life. Spiritually connected. Thank you, Lord. More than a friend. Her songs and music will bless your life as God allows her to minister to so many people. For me, because of the connection, we know when we need to connect in person. I thank God for that. She is a prayer warrior, intercessor, and blessing to many. It would take me pages to write about our friendship. She put the music to something I had written, and we always connected that way. That's our gift to each other. Do you know anyone that touches you that way? What a gift. I love her for all that she has deposited in me. If you ever want to go into the inner court, seek her out. What a blessing!! Love you, sis!! Thank you for the sisterhood!!

Marsha

This is my niece. Thank you for caring for me when I was ill. You came to my rescue many times, and I can't thank you enough. I pray for continuous blessings in your life for you and your family. She stayed with me after cancer surgery, nursing home visits, and comforting me through my recovery. She hasn't allowed me to do the same for her at this fragile moment in her life, but I love her, and I'll never forget all that she did for me. I truly love her. When your family wants to help with no strings attached, let them. Thank you for the sisterhood!!

Debbie

This is my niece. Thank you for being there when I needed to go to appointments during my critical time when I had cancer. Although you never stayed with me when I was receiving chemo, I knew you would be there to pick me up when it was completed. Do you remember the one appointment I had, we were on the elevator, and I almost lost my pants as I had lost so much weight. We just laughed. What a sight. I knew you cared about what was happening to me, although you never said anything, but that's just your personality. Thank you. Love you for that!

Almost forgot. The visit when I was in ICU, and you, Chad, came to see me and made fun of my laugh because I couldn't laugh right due to the incision. We laughed together and the nurse came in and said we were having too much fun and I was ready to go to another floor. We laughed more. Let your family in when you're going through issues in your life. They'll be there for you if you let them. Thanks for the sisterhood!!

90

Marge

When I moved to another city, there was a woman that I interviewed with at a hospital, and because of what she saw in me, she hired me to be a recruiter/interviewer. Wow! Only God. We had a good partnership going in, and I thank her for the opportunity when I didn't know anything about Human Resources, Interviewing, or Recruiting. But we know that He will equip you wherever your assignment is when you're open and willing. How many people can you think of that have given you a chance? If you haven't thanked them, it's never too late. Thank you for the sisterhood!!

Vetta/Lainy

I can only thank God for the time I got to know them. We were in ministry school together and when I left my church, they both said where I was going was a safe place to heal. I was hurting from church hurt and didn't know what to do or where to go, but I found what I needed to heal and make me whole again.

They have moved on with their lives in ministry and to another state.

I won't ever forget when Lainy came and prayed with me when I was very ill. We prayed so hard and intensely that I knew we shook up heaven. Thank you, Lord, for them being a part of my life. We should all have people who care enough to come when you need them without any questions. They were both just there for me.

Thank you both, and God Bless!! Thanks for the sisterhood!!

Ilecia

How do you describe her? She is an introvert, except with family at times. There is a woman deep inside who won't allow her to be who God has called her to be. She's an artist, nail professional, and fashionista. When God's timing is in place, she will rise to the occasion. She doesn't expose anything about herself as that is her protection from getting hurt. She has her pain and disappointments, but she has risen above all that and is on her way. She can save a penny for shopping experiences and enjoys traveling when she has the chance. She never asks anyone for help as she would rather do everything on her own, but she's learning. Everyone needs someone from time to time. She's exploring working with disadvantaged clients and I pray the best for her. She's a champ, and I love her dearly.

Be there when they reach out to listen, guide, and direct. She's exploring more and more about the word of God and where it's taking her.

Thanks for the sisterhood!!

Missy

My daughter is from another mother. I met her and her family when her son was injured and needed in-home nursing. I had planned on taking another assignment in Lebanon, but the Lord led me to her and her family. I was his caregiver for approximately 3 years but maintained our relationship for the past 15 years (I think). I acknowledge her strength, tenacity, love, caring, and faith during the years I've known her. She and her family changed my life. They became friends with my grandchildren when I would take them with me sometimes at night and had a lot of fun together. They have been through some difficult times, but they've made it and I'm so grateful for meeting them. Her children are educated and successful.

Thanks for the sisterhood!!

Jackie and Rosalind

Thanks for letting me be a part of your family and for the many stories we've shared. Thank you for the memories and the sisterhood!!

Patty

When we first met, I wasn't quite sure how we were going to be with each other as we didn't talk to each other much but had a lot in common. With God on her side, she was the winner. I just needed to be still and wait on God. We've shared many memories about our families, especially when it comes to our sisters, with tears of joy and happiness.

Her sister is in a nursing home in Alabama, and she finally got a chance to go to see her and they had a wonderful time. She is a mother, grandmother, and a true servant of the Lord. She recently passed at the wonderful age of 93.

I thank God for our relationship and the many birthdays we have yet to share.

Thank you for the sisterhood!!

Collette

This is my niece, and I thank you for coming to my aid and allowing me to stay at your home when I was ill.

Thank you for the sisterhood!!

Vette

This is my great niece by family dynamics, and she was a gem to me. She loved life, my daughter and my granddaughter Deija when she was so very young.

She lost her life early at the age of 23 and has been sorely missed for years.

She loved to talk about Michael Jordan and wanted so much to see him.

I thank God that I was able to contact his foundation, and speak with his administrative assistant, who took all of our information down, and sent her a baseball cap, a watch, a 6-foot poster of MJ, and a personalized letter from Michael. What a blessing!

She loved hard, and she and my daughter were the best of friends and at getting themselves in trouble.

What a joy. Thanks for the sisterhood and knowing and loving you!!

You must believe so that you

can receive.

Bishop Thomas

I thank God that I had an opportunity to meet a female Bishop in my lifetime.

She helped me learn more about the bible through training and studying, and I'll be forever grateful.

We butt heads on several occasions, but it was part of growing in Christ.

Many have been blessed because of her ministry. Thanks for the sisterhood!!

Yolanda

I can't thank you enough for all of the nights we worked together and laughed together. You had such care and concern for your patients, and it always showed in your work.

We shared stories about our families, your mom, and your family. Always a treat for me. You always encouraged me as I made buttons and coffee mugs, exemplifying caregivers.

I will never forget you, and thanks for keeping in touch on Facebook. Thanks for the surprise visit when I was being celebrated at church...Love you, sis.

Thanks for the sisterhood!!

Jeremiah

Not really her name, but the name she gave her Shofar.

I met her on my way to a Juanita Bynum conference in Atlanta. What a time on that plane.

She was a server to Juanita to make sure people were properly seated and to control the crowd as Juanita was ministering. Who would have thought? That was in 2004.

Every time I went to a Juanita Bynum conference in California, and other cities, she was there.

It was God ordained getting to know one another and discussing the sessions. I was overwhelmed.

She came to visit one Saturday at a previous church, and she blew the Shofar to bless the house. It was awesome.

Although we don't see each other anymore, we still touch base on FB, and I was so excited for her when she became an Elder.

She has a ministry of intercession that makes sure intercessors are giving God their all no matter what the circumstances and staying committed.

Love ya sis. Thanks for the sisterhood!!!

Carla

Thank you for who you are in Christ. All the meals you have prepared, your willingness to always lend a helping hand, and your love for the people.

Create your vision board of how you want your soup kitchen to look and watch God work. 'Don't talk about it, Be about it' this year. This is your year to MOVE.

I admonish all that you do to help others by taking them in and giving them a place to stay. You provided words of encouragement to help them along their way. It takes someone special to reach out to others as you do.

Thank you for the Sisterhood!!

Terry

Rising from the ashes where you were when you were in the world to where you are today is only because of prayer and God's will for your life. Don't disappoint Him or yourself.

Keep striving, keep teaching, reaching and being an example for others.

God never said it would be easy, but He did say, 'I'll never leave you nor forsake' you. Get your vision board back out and watch God work. Make sure you hear what He and He alone is saying.

Thank you for the sisterhood!!

Pastor Linder

Sweet Woman of God

I can't begin to thank her for all that she has contributed to my life.

She is always encouraging, uplifting, and obedient to the word of the Lord.

She is a true woman of God. She exemplifies the words faithful and committed to the cause of Christ.

I am so grateful for her being a part of my life. I wish nothing but the best of God's blessings for her and her family.

Thank you for the sisterhood

Won't He Do It

How awesome are these words
Won't He do it just for me
But they apply to everyone
Who has faith and just believes.
How many times have you sought Him
And He answered as He does
For He is our provider
As He surrounds us with His love.
He says not to worry
Just cast our cares on Him
He'll never leave us
Nor forsake us
He is our loving friend.
So when He has blessed you
Make sure you let Him know
How much you truly love Him
And all the grace He has shown.

My famous words are "Won't He Do It"

Reflections of Sisterhood. Be blessed!!!

Tanise

I couldn't believe how much praise dancing changed the atmosphere until you came and finally began using the gift that God had placed within you.

I so appreciate how each dance ministers to me, and His people and I thank you. I've seen the dancers' lives changing as their commitment to Christ is demonstrated in their dance.

Thank you for the sisterhood

Rosy

How could I not thank you enough for your songs on the prayer line?

I so appreciate your testimony and prayers that are sent up, as they always bless my soul.

Thank you for being who you are in my life and for the joy you bring.

Stay encouraged as God continues to work with you and yours through Jesus Christ.

Thank you for the Sisterhood.

I think I spelled Rosy correctly. (big smile)

Sharon

I met her online several years ago as I asked God to send me a mentor to help with my walk.

As I was surfing Facebook, I saw this bible study for women by Sharon Gill and decided to write to her and ask her if she would consider being a mentor to me. Encouragement, guidance, and direction. Always to Christ and not to herself.

We wrote several times to each other, and she said yes, and we've been writing every since.

We shared whatever God had spoken to each other, and it has been a wonderful, enlightening time in the Lord.

She was not judgmental in wanting to know why. She just listened.

As we shared, I watched her ministry grow and grow. Her speaking engagements were growing as well. I pray that one day, I'll be able to bring her here.

During this time, her mother passed, and she encountered some health issues. It didn't stop her. With her husband, family, and friends, she continued her journey. Always wanting to empower women for the cause of Christ. What a joy for me!!

I spoke to her about having a conference, and she finally did it. Praise God.

I thank God for her as she continues on the path God has designed for her and her family. Nobody but you, Lord, Nobody but you.

Thank you for the sisterhood.

First Lady

I didn't realize how difficult it is to be the First Lady of a church until I took an intricate look at the First Lady.

It's a difficult task because you have to be everything to everybody, including your husband,

Expectations are high, but when she and I finally got on one accord I understood much more.

I'm grateful for the time we've spent doing projects, praying, and uplifting the name of the Lord. The encouragement and inspiration you've shared with me will never be forgotten. Thanks for the Sisterhood.

Pastor Abdullah

Words cannot express how I feel except to say Thank you. You know the rest.

What a blessing you are now a Bishop -- congratulations.

Thank You!

Keep an eye out for the upcoming release of

"I REPRESENT POSSIBILITIES,"

A transformative book that promises to inspire and ignite new horizons!